Landmarks

by Hei

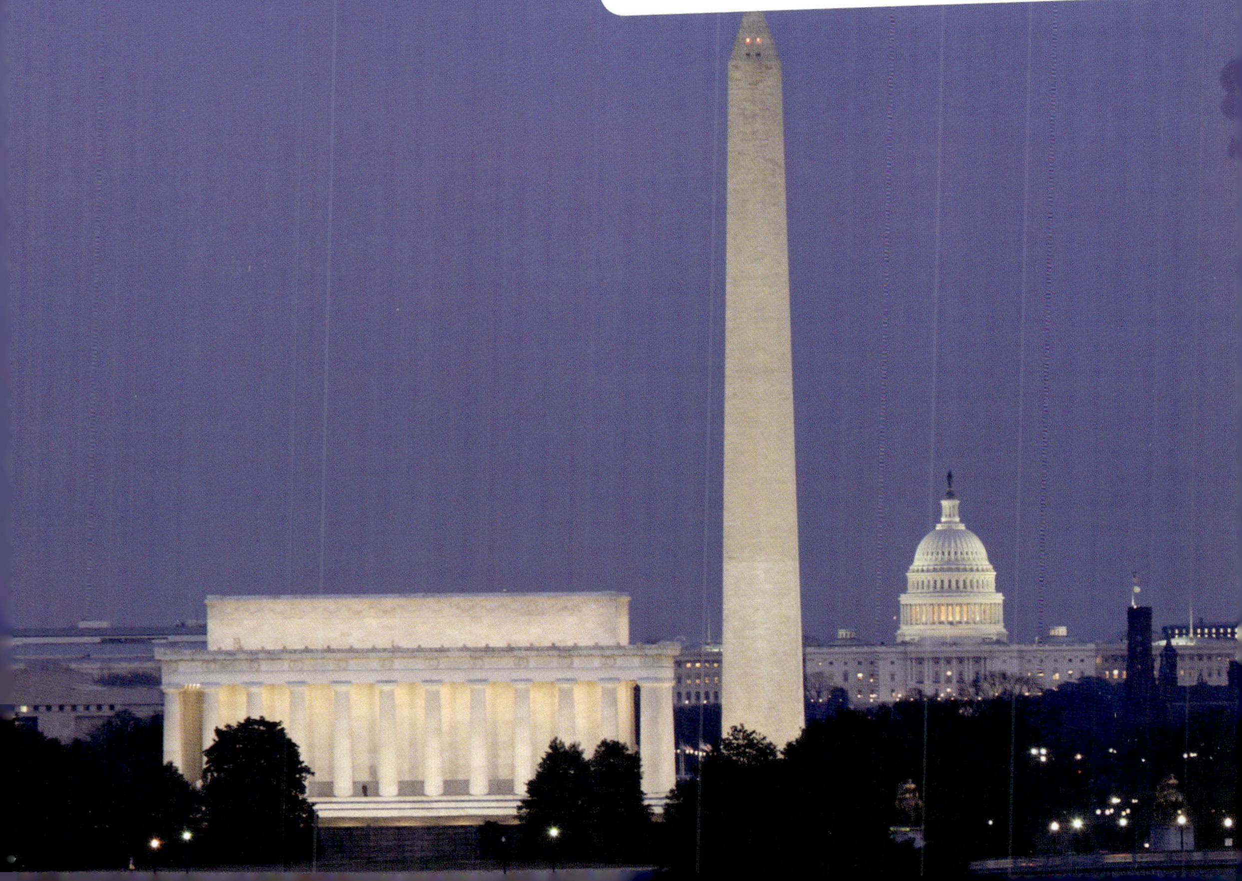

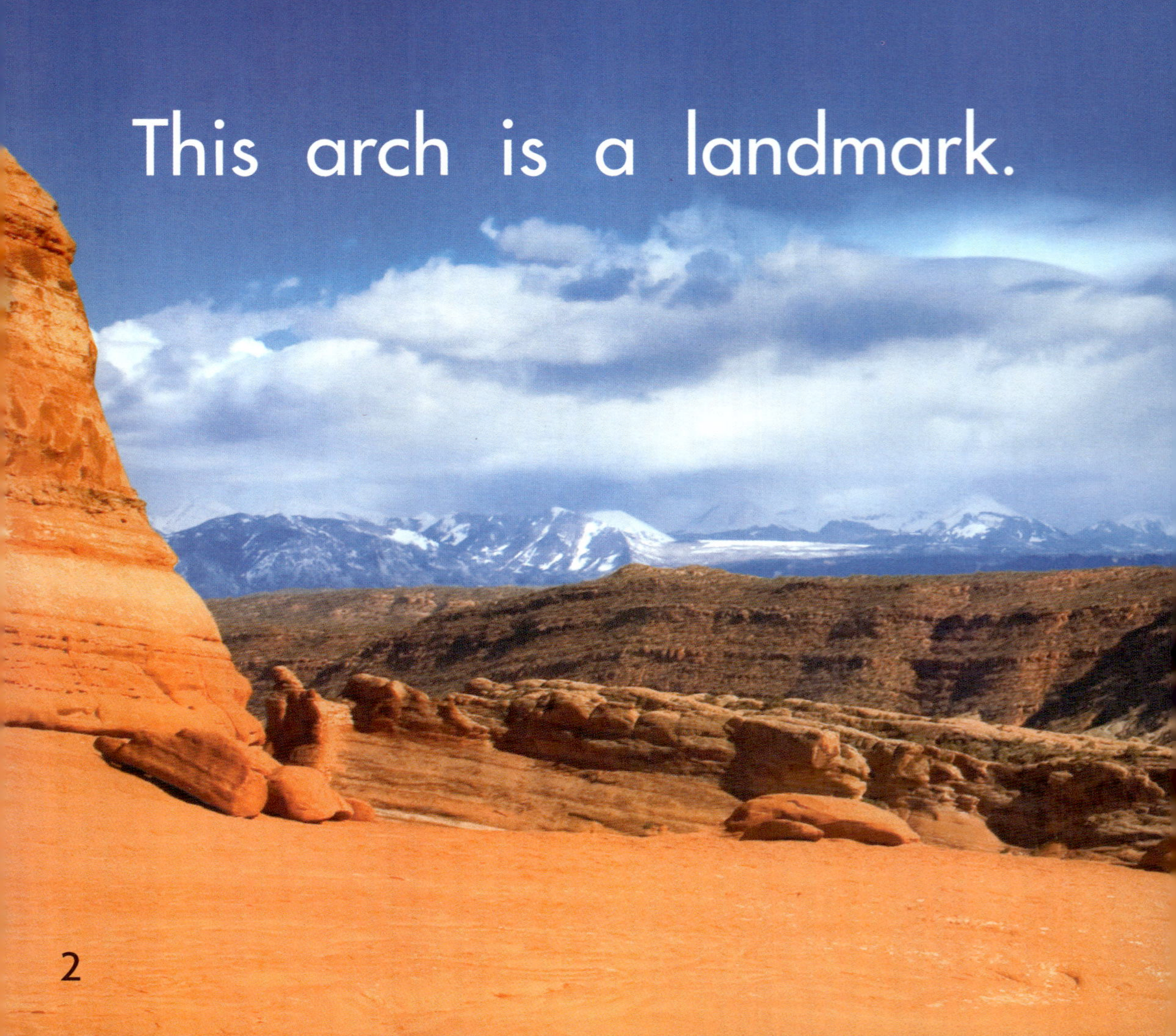

This arch is a landmark.

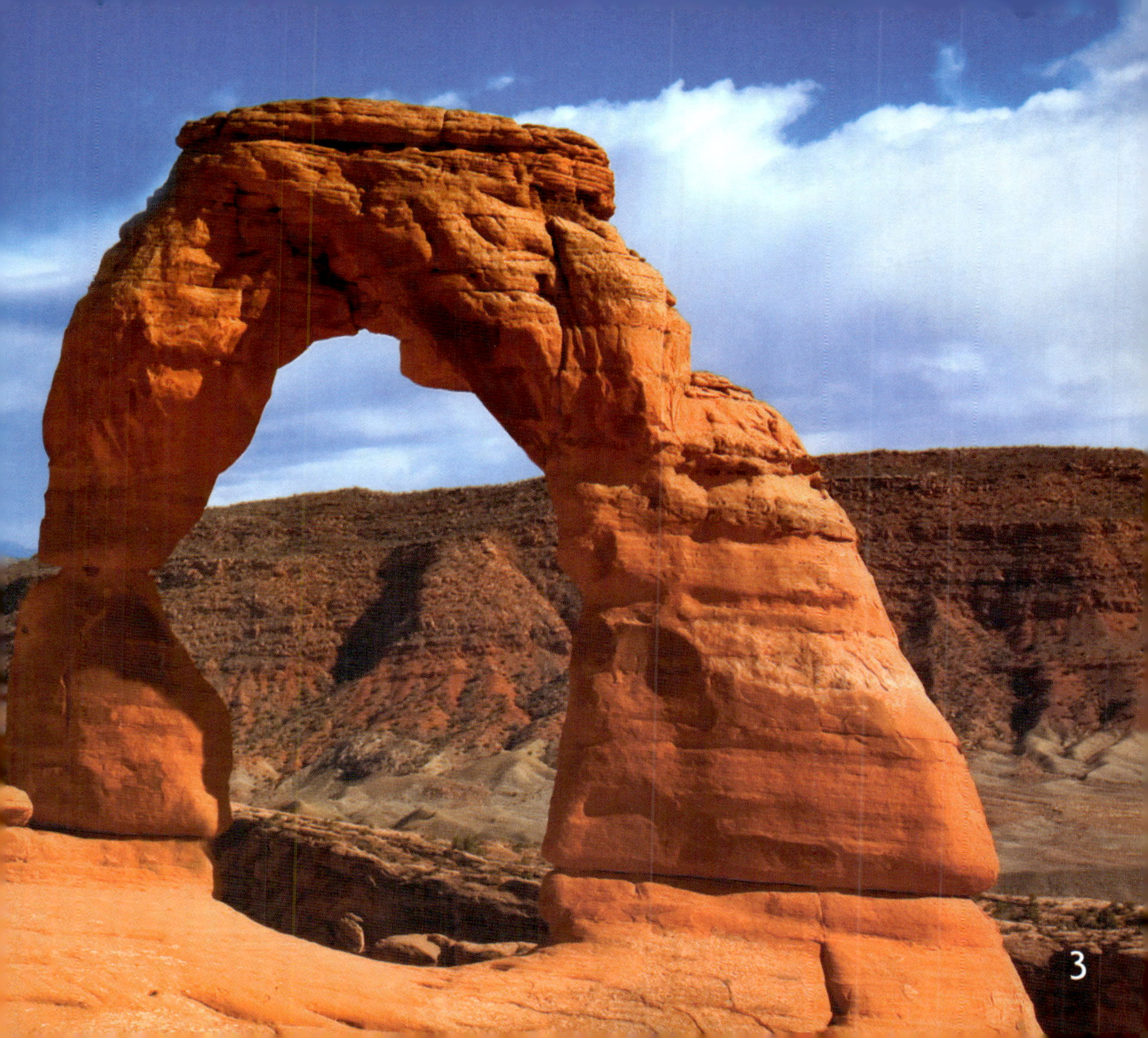

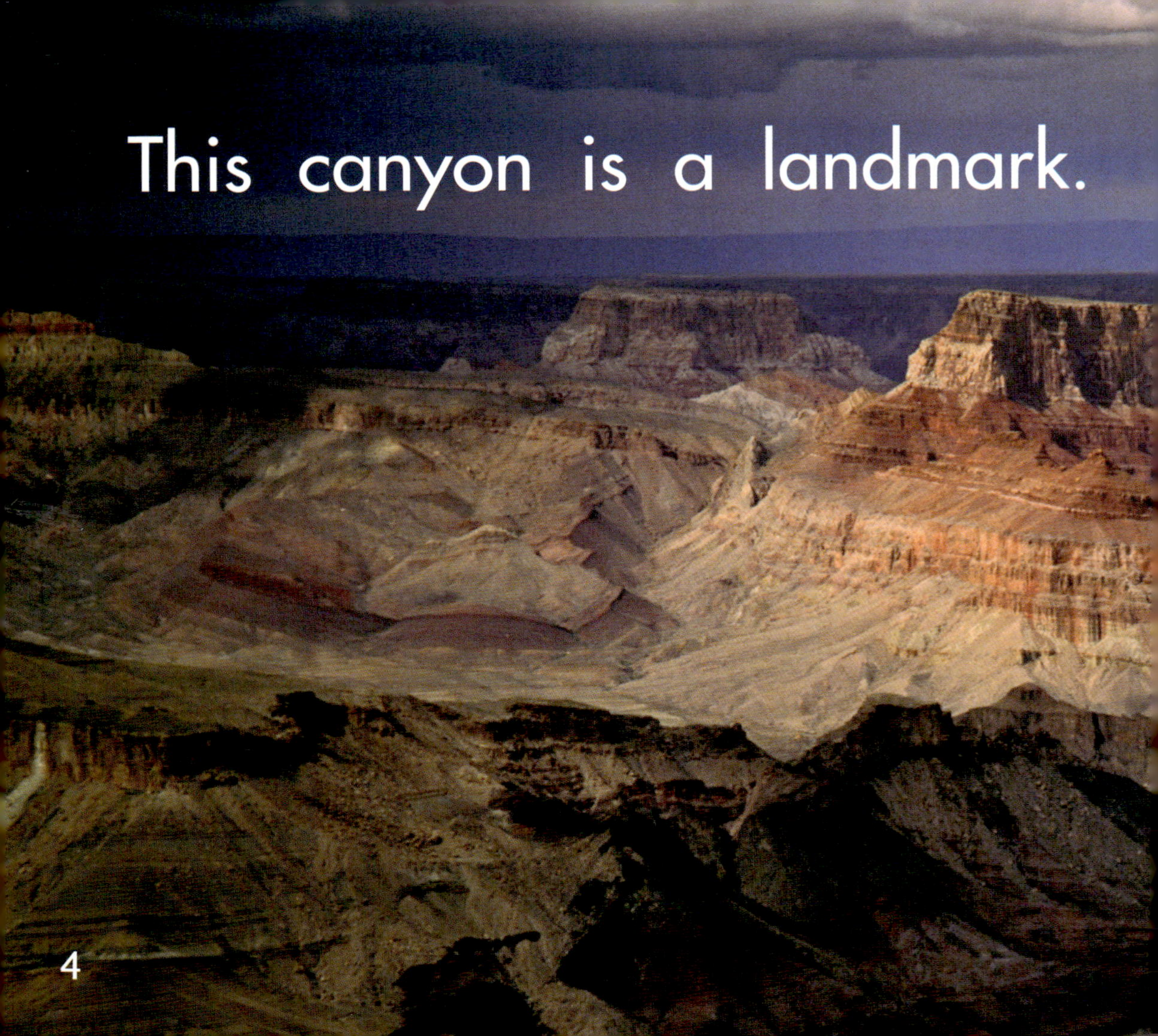

This canyon is a landmark.

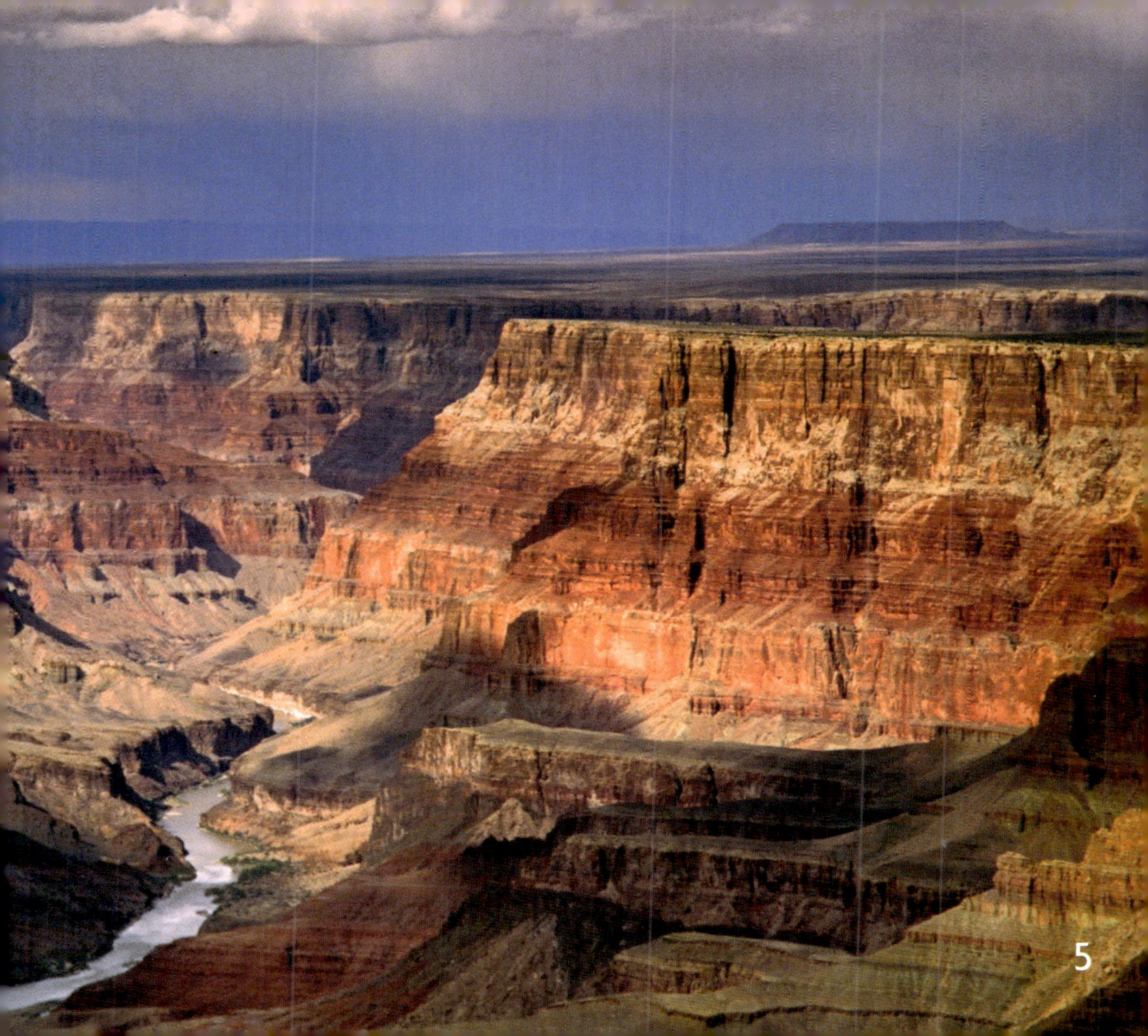

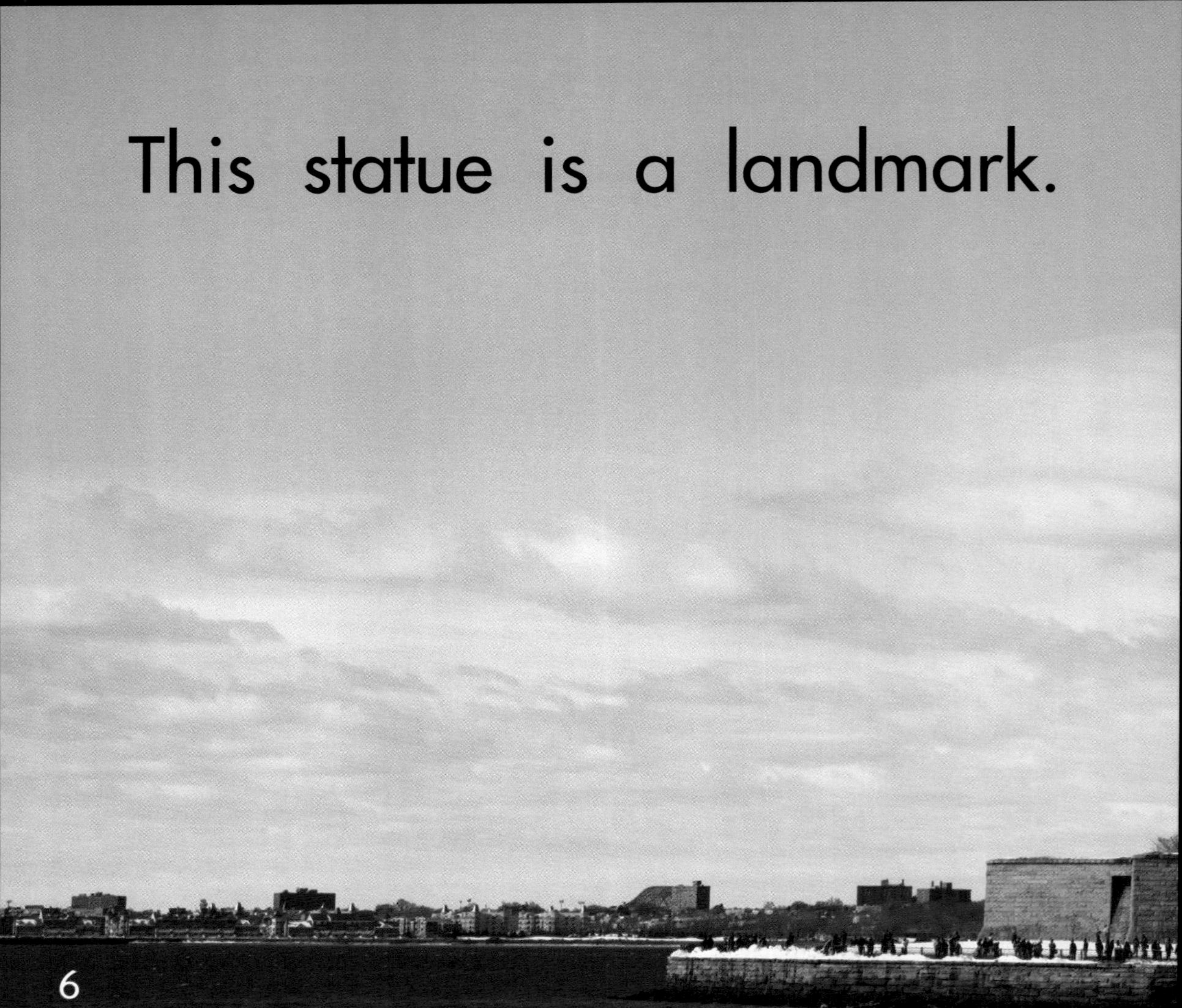

This statue is a landmark.

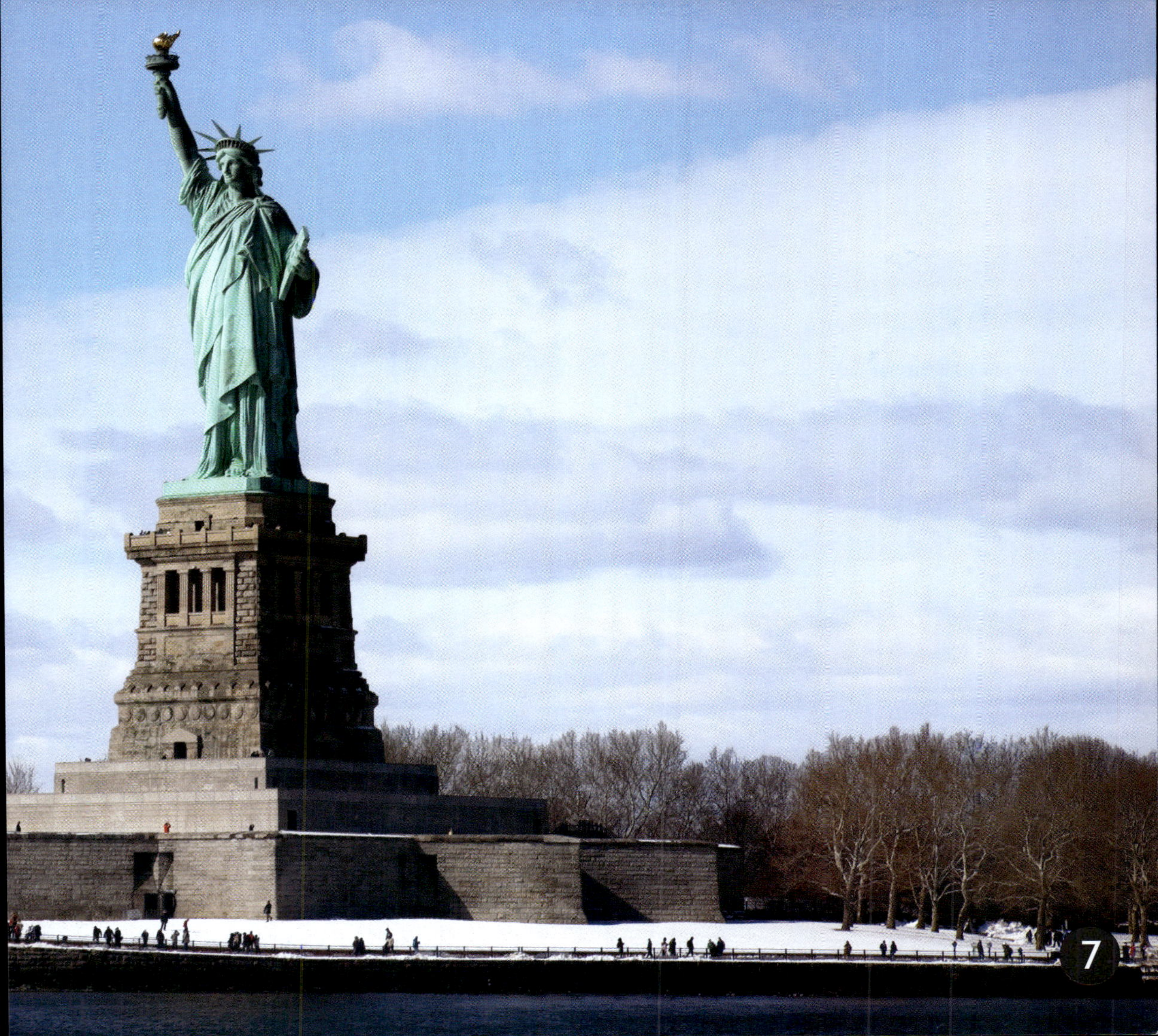

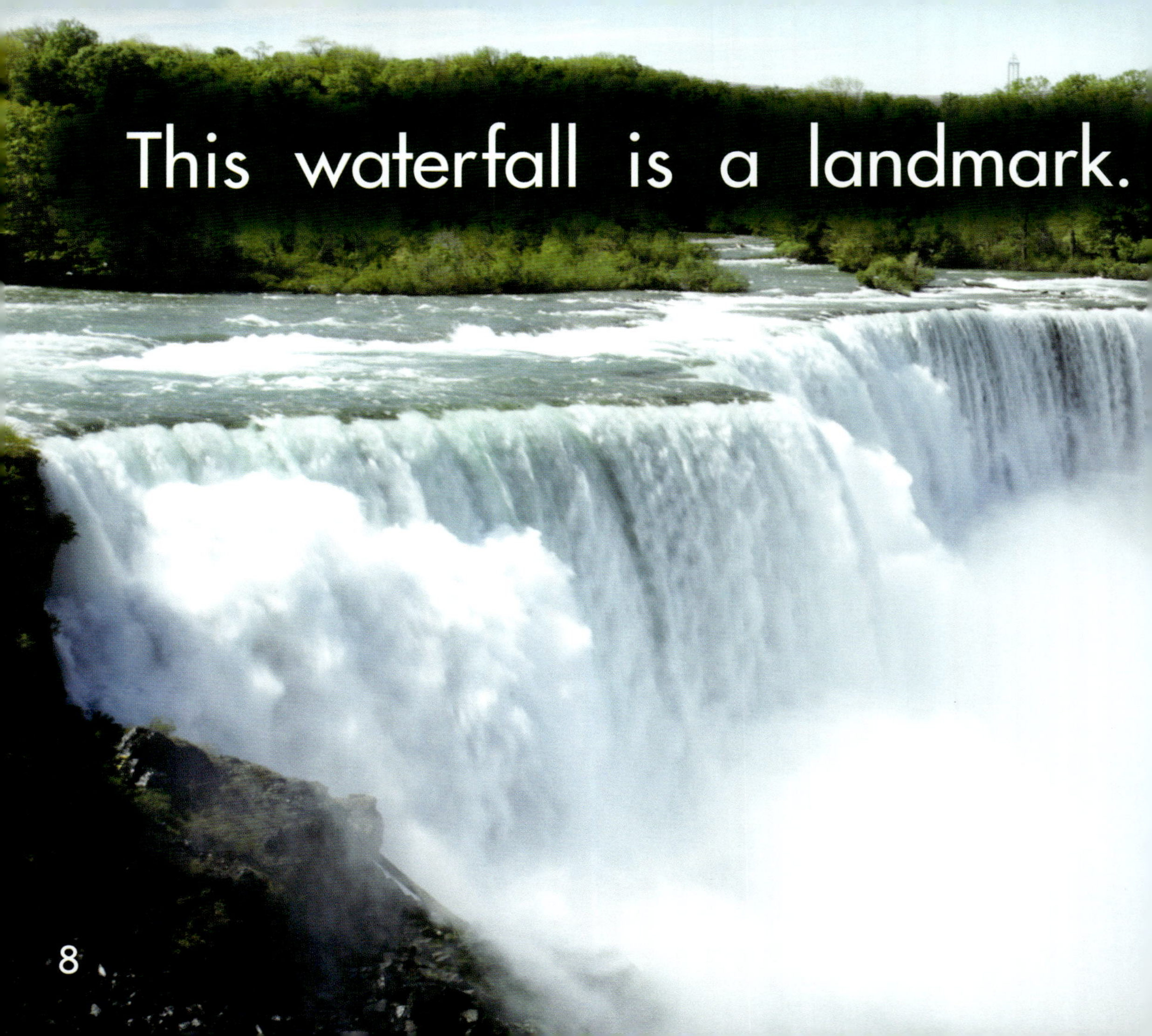
This waterfall is a landmark.

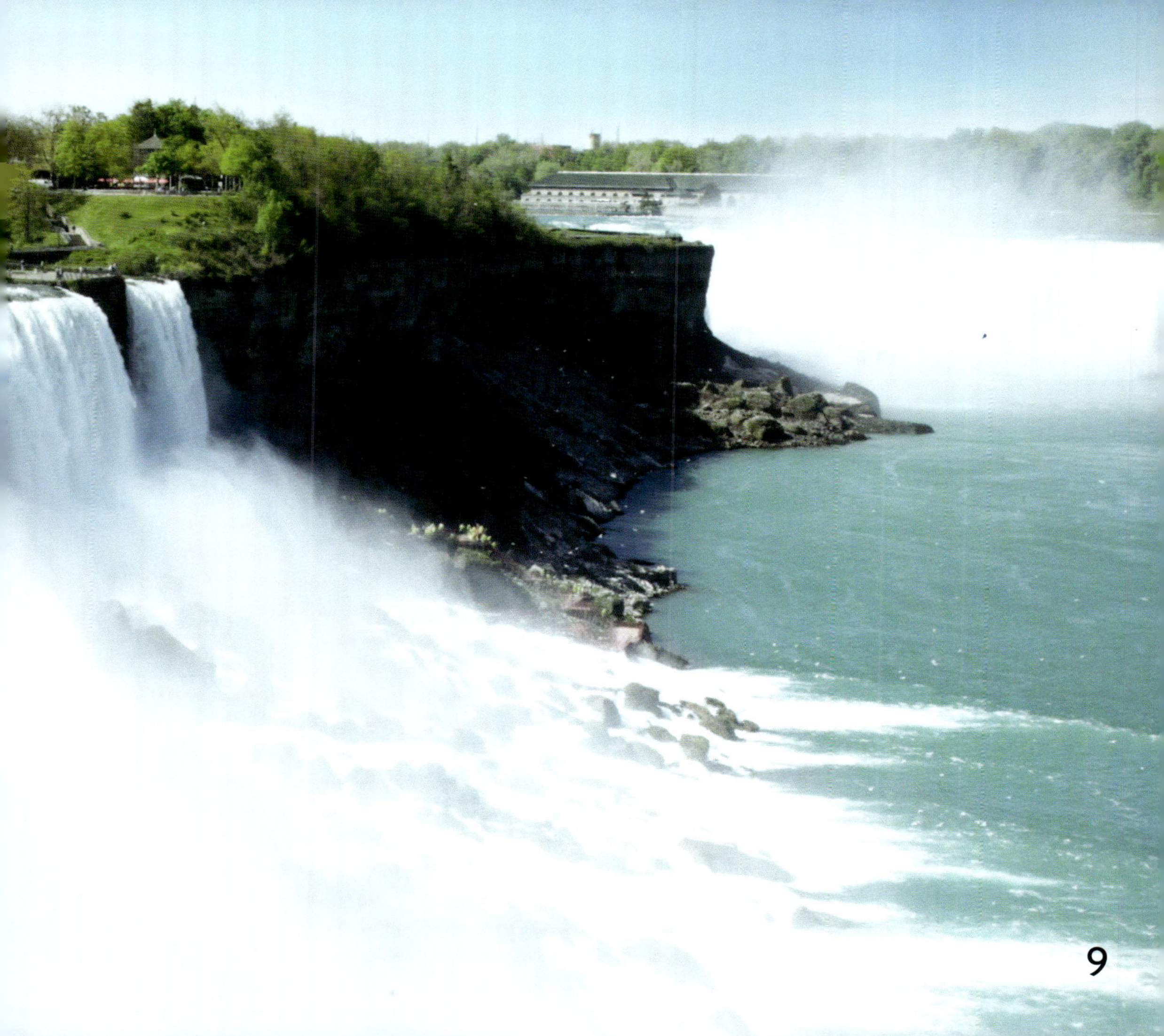

This sign is a landmark.

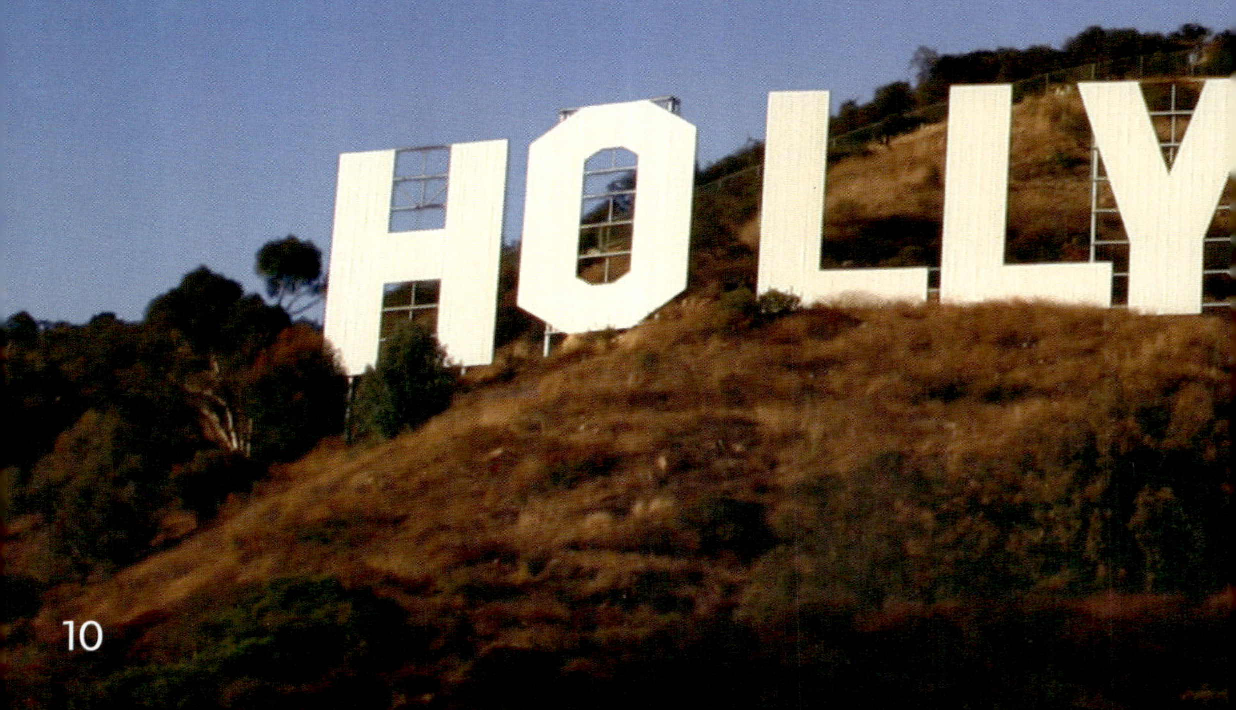

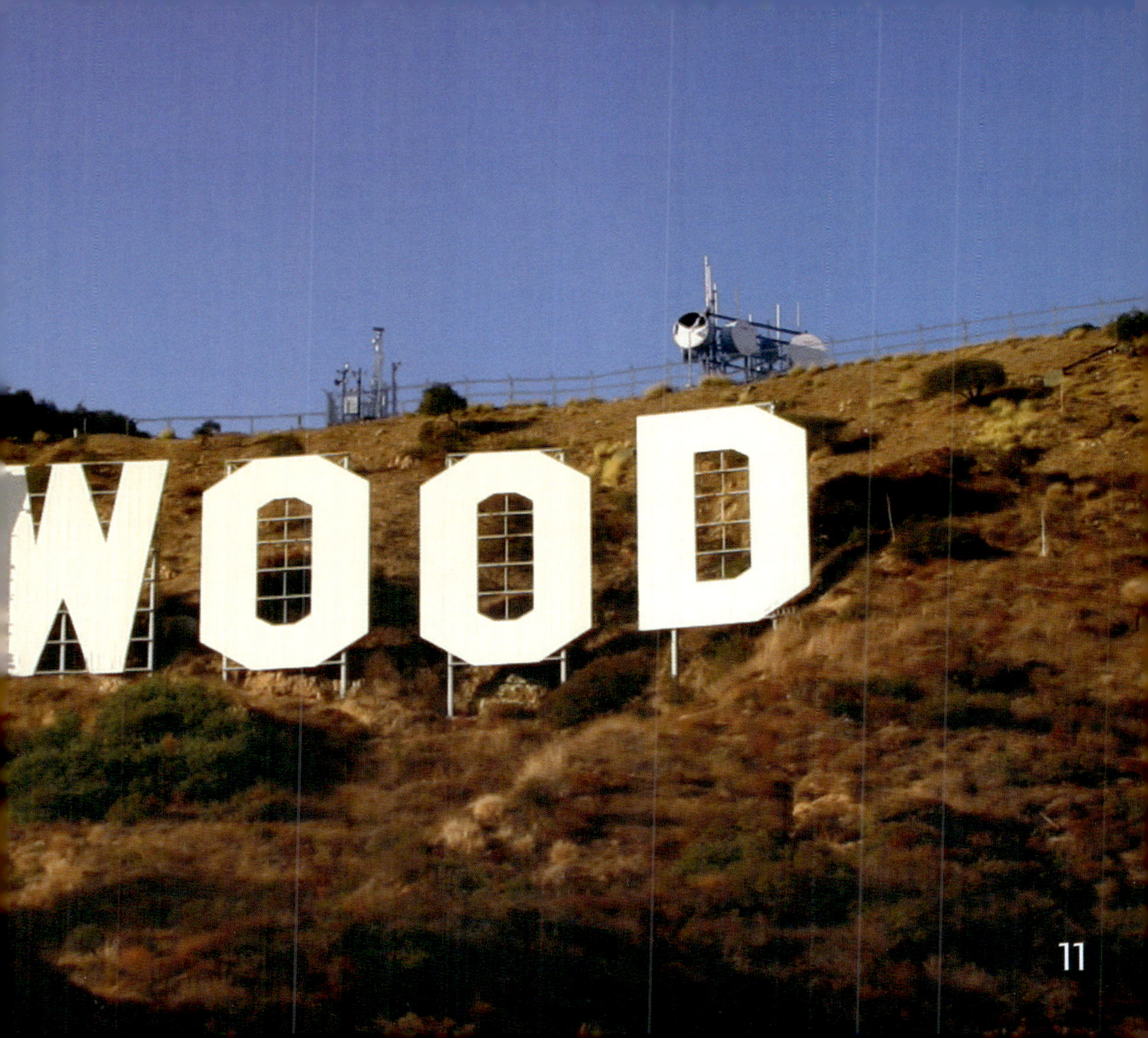
WOOD

This river is a landmark.

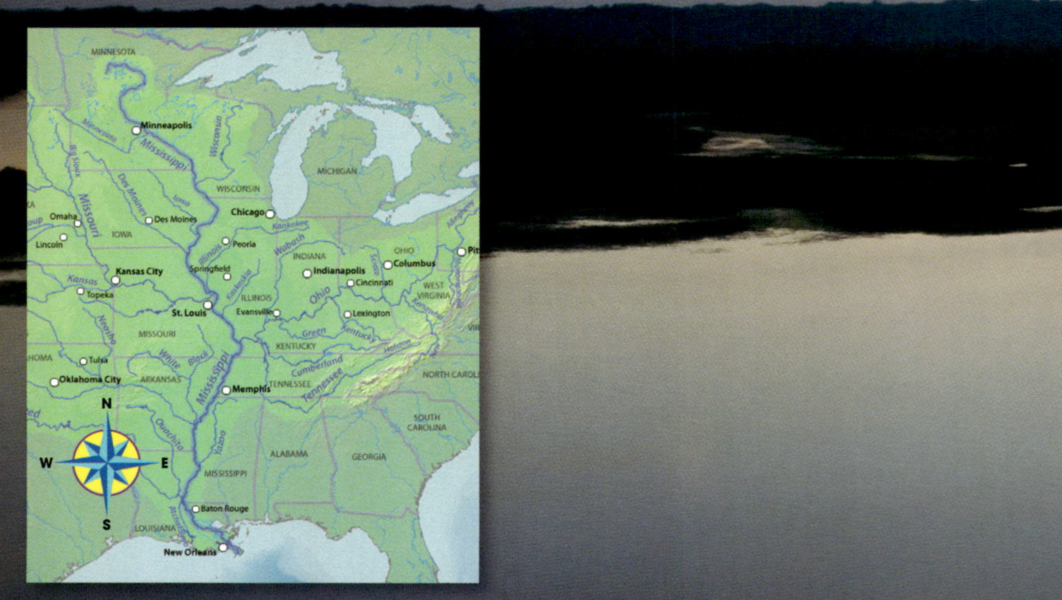

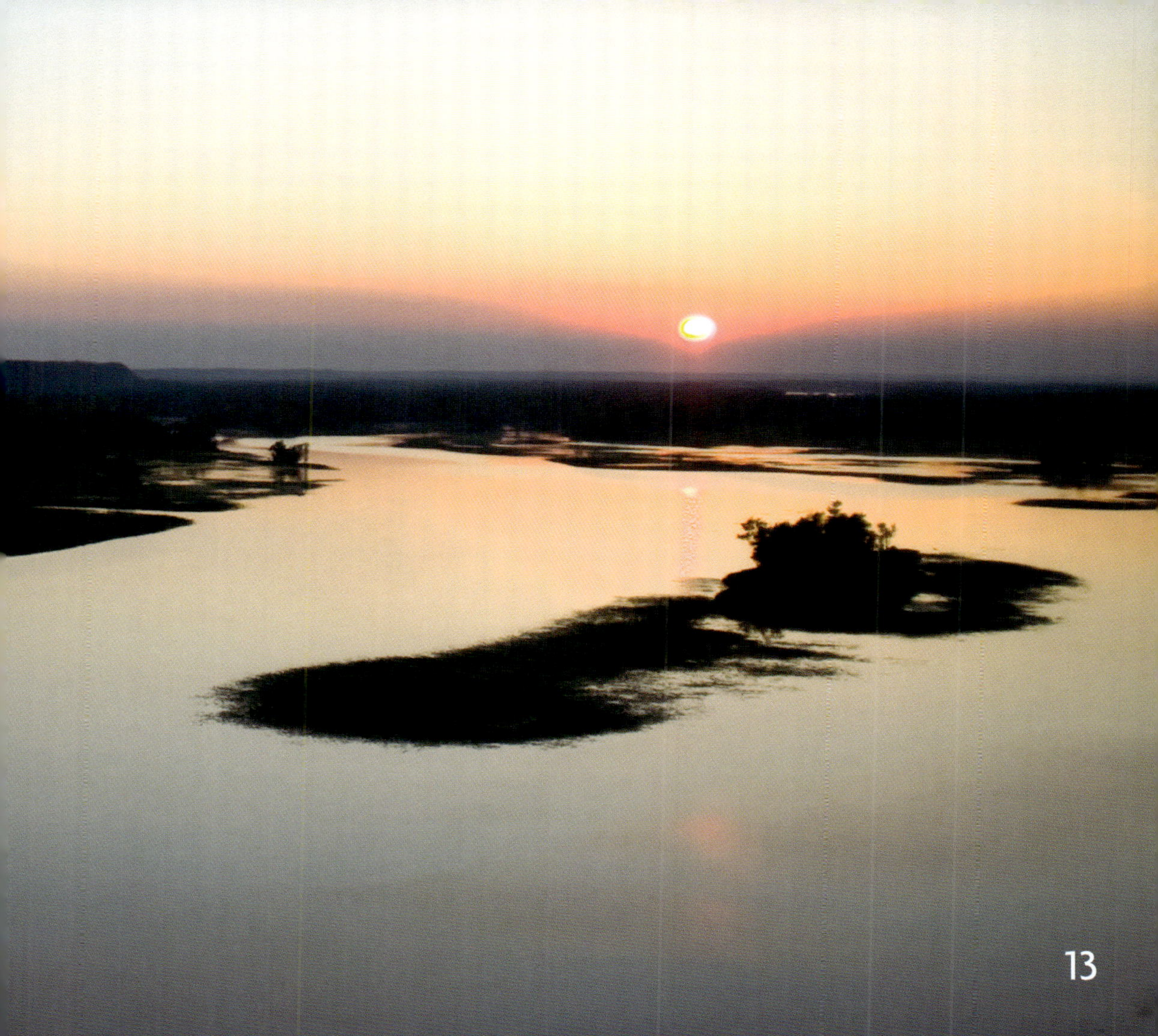

This building is a landmark.

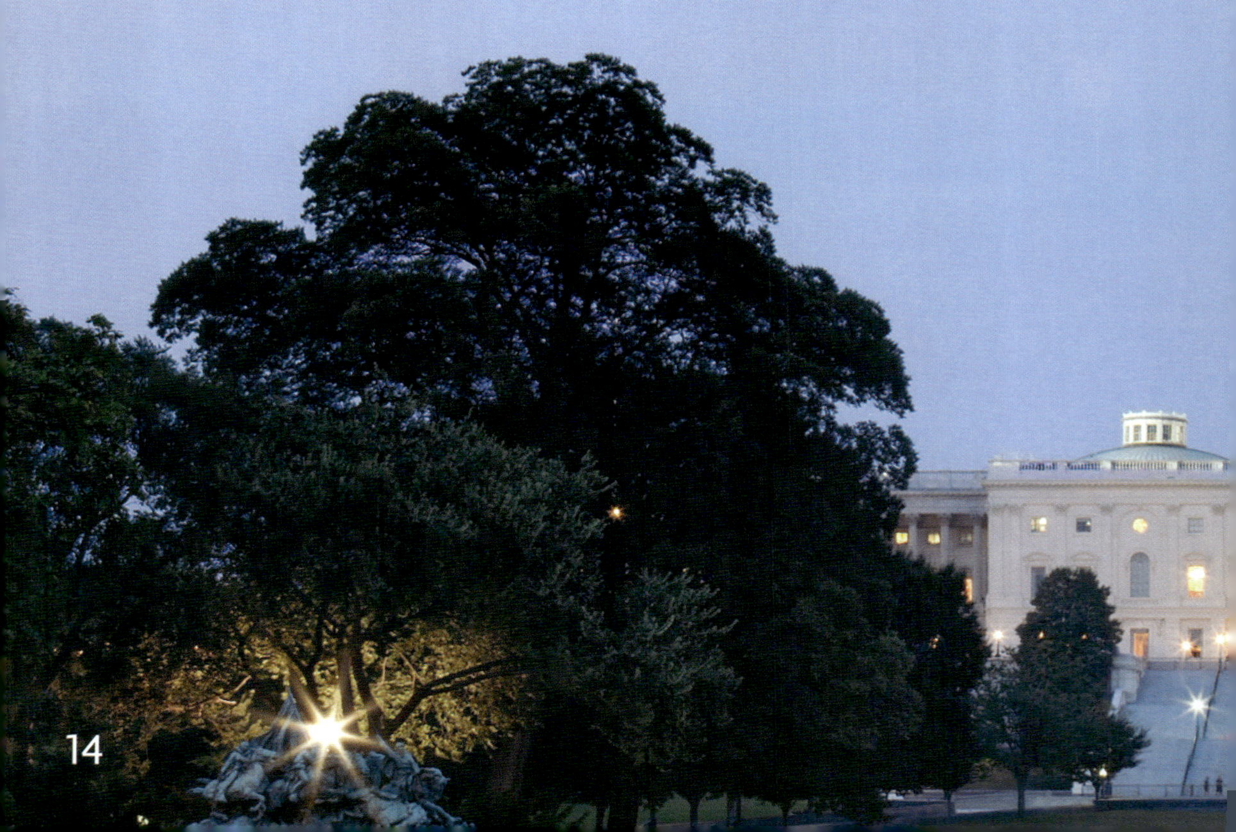

14

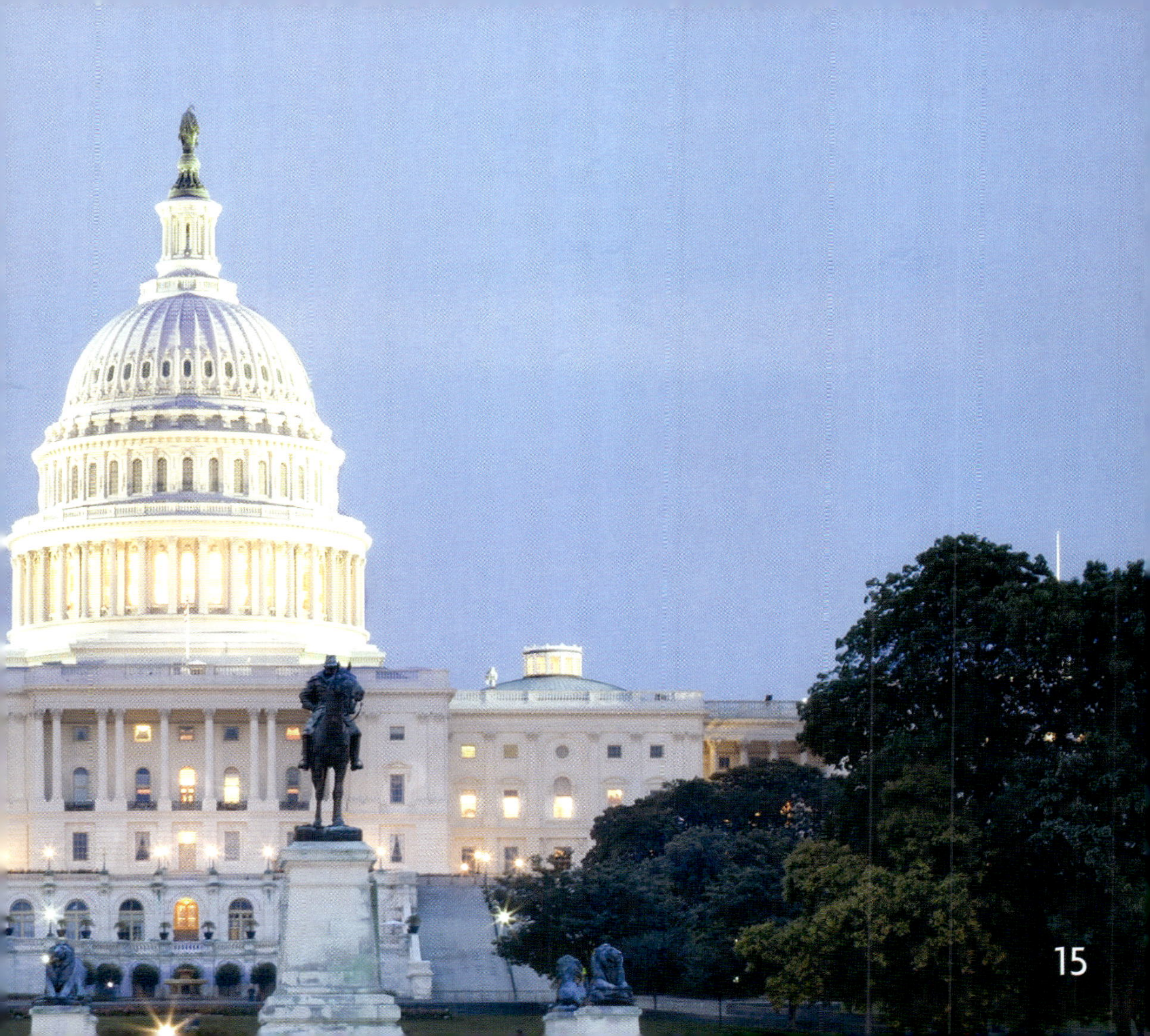

The U.S.A. has landmarks!

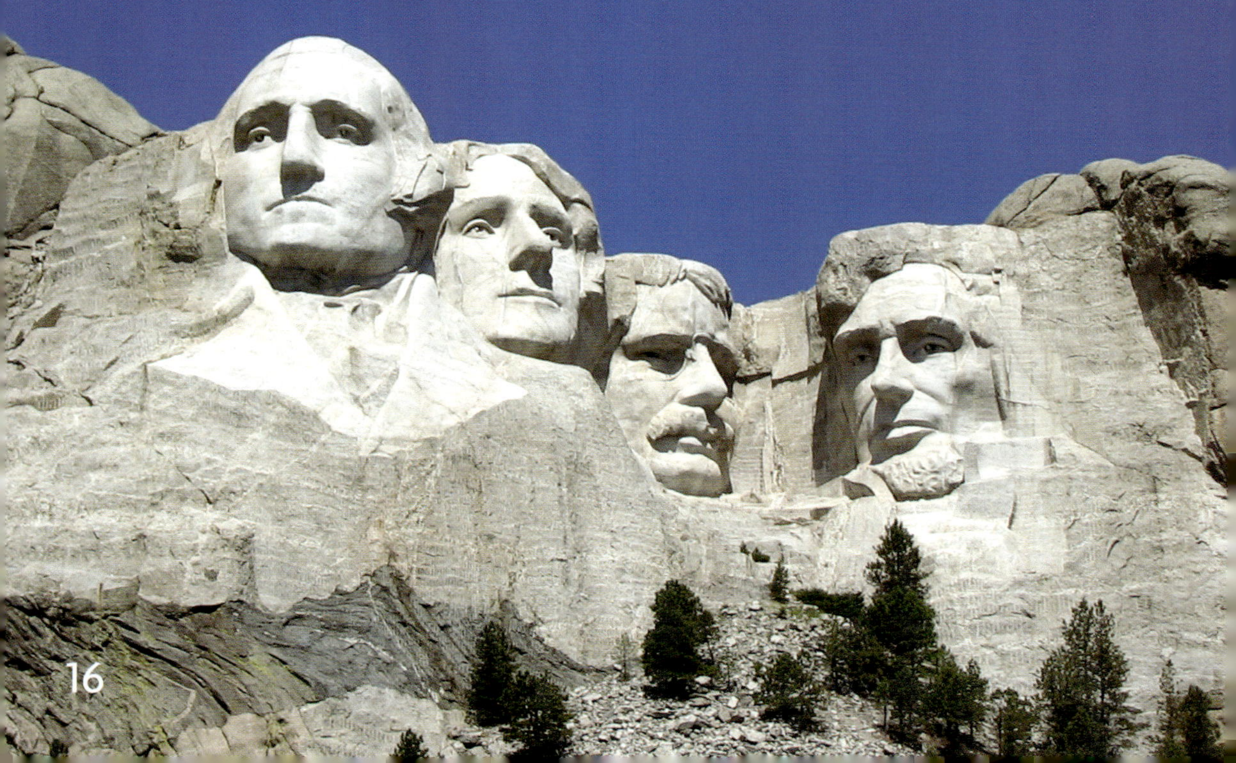